11/13/14

# CLIMATE CRISIS

# People

## Stephen Aitken

Cavendish
Square

New York

Louisburg Library
Bringing People and Information Together

*Special thanks to Jamison Ervin, a conservation specialist and a project manager with the United Nations Development Programme, for her expert review of this manuscript.*

Published in 2014 by Cavendish Square Publishing, LLC
303 Park Avenue South, Suite 1247, New York, NY 10010

Library of Congress Cataloging-in-Publication Data
Aitken, Stephen, 1953–
People / Stephen Aitken.
    p.   cm. — (Climate crisis)
Includes bibliographical references and index.
Summary: "Provides comprehensive information on climate change and its effects on the human population"—Provided by publisher.
ISBN 978-1-60870-461-3 (hardcover)
ISBN 978-1-62712-041-8 (paperback)
ISBN 978-1-60870-632-7 (ebook)
1. Human beings—Effect of climate on—Juvenile literature. 2. Climate changes—Juvenile literature. I. Title.
GF71.A47 2013
363.738'74—dc23
2011036956

Editor: Christine Florie
Art Director: Anahid Hamparian
Series Designer: Nancy Sabato

Photo research by Laurie Platt Winfrey, Carousel Research, Inc.

Cover: Corbis/ Pete McBride, National Geographic Society

The photographs in this book are used by permission and through the courtesy of:
*Alamy*: Richard Green, Title page; dieKleinert, 11,12; Vito Arcomano, 28-29. *Associated Press*: Imagine China, 18; Brennan Linsley, 21. *Corbis*: Cindy Kassab, 8-9. *Glow Images*: Duncan Maxwell/Robert Harding, 4. *Media Bakery*: Background details. *Newscom*: Arlan Naeg/AFP/Getty, 49. *Superstock*: Wolfgang Kaehler, 7; Nomad, 14-15; Minden Pictures, 22, 30; Dave Reede/All Canada, 24, Chris Cheadle/All Canada, 34; George Ostertag, 36-37; Imagebroker.net, 39, 52-53; Yann Guichaoua, 41; John Warburton-Lee, 46-47; Steve Vidler, 55.

Printed in the United States of America

# Contents

# Introduction

limatic conditions on the earth vary widely, from the dry, frigid temperatures of the Antarctic Peninsula to the heat and humidity of the tropical rain forests of the Amazon River basin. Because of the spherical shape of the earth and its tilt as it orbits the sun, different locations on the planet receive varying amounts of sunlight and heat. In the tropics, the region around the equator, the constant direct sunlight produces high surface temperatures year round; meanwhile, the sun strikes the polar regions at such a sharp angle that they receive little direct sunlight, and thus they are cold and frozen for most of the year. The widely differing temperature regions found on the earth tend to create swirling winds because warm, moist air rises up and draws in dry, cool air underneath it. This temperature-moisture interchange in the air takes place all over the planet; it creates weather patterns that can persist for days—or change in an hour.

People have adapted to living in almost every type of climatic condition on the earth, no matter how rugged; the one exception is Antarctica, where there are no permanent human inhabitants. Climate refers to the typical weather experienced year after year at a given location, in a given season. The climate in Florida is usually sunny

Most researchers and scientists who study the changes taking place in earth's climate believe that much of that change is due to human activities, such as the burning of fossil fuels as seen here at oil refineries in Scotland.

and warm. Cold and freezing temperatures are the norm in Alaska in December. Climate is something that has come to be thought of as more or less predictable, but how fixed is the earth's climate?

According to geological and **ice core** data, the earth's climate has changed many times over the planet's 4-billion-year history—even since the end of the last ice age, 12,000 years ago—and it is undergoing a major change now. Most present-day climatologists are convinced that the rise in the earth's temperature recorded over the last 150 years, commonly referred to as global warming, is largely the result of human activities. The term *climate change* refers to global warming and all the additional changes that have occurred as a result of the temperature increase, including changing patterns of rainfall and snow; an increase in extreme weather events such as tornadoes, hurricanes, and cyclones; range shifts in animals and plants; and an increase in **invasive species**. What is both unique and disturbing about the current warming of the planet is the rate at which it is taking place and its effect on human populations and living conditions all over the world.

At the time modern humans appeared on the earth, about 200,000 years ago, evolutionary processes had been taking place for billions of years. Ecosystems were well established, soils were fertile, and there was freshwater in the lakes and rivers. Trees grew in extensive forests that spread across continents and helped to regulate the planet's climate. Humans found the forests and grasslands to be good hunting grounds for prey as well as good sources of fruits, berries, and other plant foods.

After tens of thousands of years of a wandering lifestyle, humans settled down. They started growing their own food and raising livestock.

They chopped down forests for fuel and built shelters. They developed the newly cleared land into fields for the cultivation of food crops and as grazing land for livestock. For the first time, humans produced food surpluses.

People figured out how to dig deep pockets into the earth to access its liquid energy, oil. This black treasure propelled society into a new era of freedom—freedom from dependence on human physical labor. A gallon of gas dramatically increased work output and gave humans the ability to accomplish

Climate change has contributed to fluctuating rainfall patterns, with some regions experiencing dramatic increases, resulting in widespread flooding.

tasks at a rate only dreamed of before. Access to oil, the product of ancient plankton and algae that had settled to the bottom of lakes and oceans millions of years ago, created change more radical than that seen by all previous generations put together.

From oil refineries and the products of oil came carbon dioxide and other greenhouse gases; their effects, along with those of deforestation, land-use change, and the use of coal to generate power, resulted in rising global temperatures. Within a relatively short period of time, humans had become both the perpetrators and the victims of a new problem, the onset of human-induced global climate change.

For thousands of years the earth has provided humans with bountiful agriculture, largely due to the planet's reliable, comfortable surface temperature.

## Chapter One

# The Carbon Dioxide Thermostat

Up until 600 million years ago, oxygen-dependent life-forms were only microscopic in size. Eventually, plants and other organisms emitted enough oxygen ($O_2$) into the air to create an atmosphere that could support large oxygen-breathing creatures, including humans. Many changes in climate have occurred over the course of the earth's history, but in the last ten thousand years, the thermostat on the planet has been set at a very comfortable temperature for human civilization to prosper— an average surface temperature of 57 degrees Fahrenheit (14°C).

Because of this relative comfort, humans have been able to plant crops, breed livestock, build cities, and in short, develop an advanced civilization.

The thermostat that controls the earth's temperature is both highly complex and delicate at the same time. At the very base of it is a colorless, odorless gas called carbon dioxide ($CO_2$).

## The Carbon Cycle

All life-forms contain carbon. There are approximately one trillion tons of carbon stored in the **biosphere**. Carbon enters the soil from the decomposition of plants and animals. When this carbon combines with other elements, it becomes sediment, oil, shale, and carbonate rocks. The oceans are a huge **carbon sink**. As the oceans absorb $CO_2$ from the air, the carbon finds its way into marine life and eventually reaches the ocean floor.

Studies show that when atmospheric $CO_2$ levels increase, global temperatures rise shortly thereafter. When $CO_2$ levels fall, the earth cools. This pattern has been demonstrated by numerous geological records. How does such a common, simple gas change the earth's climate?

## The Greenhouse Effect

Carbon dioxide is a **greenhouse gas**. Other greenhouse gases include water vapor, methane, and nitrous oxide. These gases trap **infrared heat** from the sun. The trapping of heat, referred to as the greenhouse effect, warms the lower atmosphere, a perfectly natural phenomenon in principle. Without greenhouse gases, much of the sun's energy would escape back into space, and the earth would be too cold to accommodate human beings and other living animals and plants.

This graphic illustrates the carbon cycle, which is the circulation of carbon atoms through our modern world.

The greenhouse effect occurs when heat from the rays of the sun strike the earth's surface. Depending on the surface they strike, a certain amount of radiant energy (or heat) is reflected back into the atmosphere as infrared rays. Ice and snow reflect more; rough, dark surfaces reflect less. The greenhouse gases form a layer in the atmosphere that traps some heat; as the heat is radiated back to the earth, the global surface temperature rises. The same occurs in a greenhouse. The light that comes in through the glass panels traps heat inside the greenhouse. The heat that is generated enables plants to be grown even when the weather outside is cold and blustery.

$CO_2$ is the most abundant of all the greenhouse gases, despite the fact that for every ten thousand molecules of atmosphere, only four are $CO_2$ molecules. $CO_2$ stays in the atmosphere for up to a hundred years. More than

As the concentration of greenhouse gases increases in the earth's atmosphere, more heat is trapped, putting upward pressure on earth's average temperature.

half of all human-generated $CO_2$ is still floating around in the atmosphere. $CO_2$ has a great influence on the ability of the atmosphere to hold water vapor. As $CO_2$ levels increase in the atmosphere, more water vapor is retained and more heat is trapped, resulting in a rise in global surface temperature.

Human beings are in the unique position of both being victimized by rising atmospheric temperatures and at the same time being the greatest producer of $CO_2$ that has ever lived on the planet. As a result many societies are beginning to question their lifestyles, their economic models, their goals, and the very definition of economic growth.

# The Keeling Curve

In 1958 a climatologist named Charles Keeling climbed to the top of the world's largest volcano, Mauna Loa, in Hawaii, in search of pure air in order to record atmospheric $CO_2$ levels. He collected data over a period of fifty years and used it to plot a graph, which became known as the Keeling curve. The fluctuations in the graph are like a snapshot of the earth's seasonal breathing patterns. Spring greenery in the Northern Hemisphere draws $CO_2$ out of the atmosphere—the earth is breathing in—and so the $CO_2$ concentration in the atmosphere falls. In the autumn months, as leaves fall and decompose, $CO_2$ is released, and the levels in the atmosphere increase—the earth is breathing out. Keeling made another important observation. He noted that each exhalation ended with slightly more $CO_2$ in the atmosphere than on the previous exhalation. The Keeling curve shows a slow, steady rise in atmospheric carbon dioxide levels over time. The 280 parts per million (ppm) that existed in the early part of the last century rose to 380 ppm by the start of this century and had reached over 390 ppm by 2011. $CO_2$ levels in the atmosphere keep increasing because very few $CO_2$ molecules leave or break down.

Prior to Keeling's work, it was not known whether $CO_2$ released from the burning of fossil fuels and other industrial activities would accumulate in the atmosphere or be fully absorbed by the oceans and vegetation on land. Keeling's measurements set the stage for today's concerns about climate change by providing one of the most important environmental data sets recorded in the twentieth century.

Downtown Los Angeles, California, is seen
shrouded in smog as a result of vehicle emissions.

## Chapter Two

# People in Greenhouses Shouldn't Throw Stones

**Many human activities contribute to the** increase in greenhouse gases in the atmosphere. Deforestation causes the release of $CO_2$, as does the burning of fossil fuels such as coal, natural gas, and petroleum for vehicles. Fossil fuels are also used to grow crops, make fertilizer, irrigate fields, and to package, ship, refrigerate, and cook the food that people eat.

# Extreme Weather Events

Scientists believe that human-caused polluting agents such as greenhouse gases and **CFCs** (chlorofluorocarbons, ozone-destroying chemicals) have caused changes in the upper levels of the earth's atmosphere. If indications that the **troposphere** is rising higher, becoming warmer, and holding more water vapor are correct, these changes may explain changes in global weather patterns.

Examples of extreme weather events have not been hard to find over the past fifteen years. The years 1997 and 1998 saw the most powerful El Niño (the warming of the ocean current along the coast of South America that is generally associated with dramatic changes in weather patterns) in recorded history. In 1998 Hurricane Mitch became famous as "the most fatal hurricane" in two hundred years. The hottest European summer on record occurred in 2003, and 2005 may go down in history as the year of the most economically devastating hurricane ever—Katrina. In 2007 flooding devastated Myanmar, and farther north, more sea ice melted than ever before in recorded history. These extreme weather events are exactly what scientists predicted would be the result of a rapidly warming atmosphere.

So what is the mechanism of global warming that causes extreme weather events? It all comes down to a very simple substance—water vapor. For every 18-degree F (10-degree C) rise in air temperature, the capacity of the air to hold water vapor doubles. Warm ocean water rapidly giving off water vapor fuels hurricanes. These conditions can transform a tropical storm into a hurricane, or transform a category 1 storm, which has winds between 74 and 95 miles per hour (119–153 kph), into a category 5 storm, where winds exceed 155 miles per hour (249 kph). The number of category 4 and category 5 storms has almost doubled since 1974, from ten a year to almost eighteen a year. Colder air does not hold as much moisture, so hurricanes do not occur in the winter months. A significant increase in the number and intensity of hurricanes is expected in the coming years.

An equally dangerous effect of extreme weather is flooding. Annual flooding affected about 7 million people in the 1960s; extreme weather pushed that number up to 150 million by the year 2005. At the end of August 2005, Katrina struck southeastern Louisiana, New Orleans in particular, with a force that resulted in more than 1,836 deaths. It was the costliest hurricane in U.S. history, with an estimated $108 billion in damages. Just 7 years later, Superstorm Sandy hit the northeastern coast of the U.S. According to a 2013 National Hurricane Centre report there were 159 lives lost and the second highest damages in U.S. hurricane history, exceeded only by Katrina.

Heat waves, on the other hand, are slow, silent killers that should never be underestimated. Extreme heat is responsible for more deaths than floods, tornadoes, and hurricanes combined. In Europe in 2003, the month of August was the hottest on record in the Northern Hemisphere. Temperatures of over 104°F (40°C) across the European continent and part of the United Kingdom resulted in more than 35,000 deaths. Climatologists predict more human deaths as extreme heat waves are likely to increase with rising global temperatures. Meteorological data shows that the sixteen warmest years on record have occurred since 1980, and the rise in global temperatures is accelerating.

# Climate Change Feedback

The Intergovernmental Panel on Climate Change (IPCC) predicts that greenhouse gas levels in the atmosphere will continue to increase this century, owing to a steady increase in carbon emissions. Computer models are used to simulate future climate conditions, and the more data is collected on the earth's changing climate and added into the models, the more confidence climatologists have in the projections. However, **climate feedback** makes those predictions difficult. Climate feedback can either increase or decrease a direct effect.

The rise in temperature that causes sea ice to melt in the Arctic is an example of a positive climate feedback. As the ice melts, the dark, exposed ocean water absorbs more solar radiation than the reflective ice surface, ultimately resulting in a rise in surface water temperature. A negative feedback, on the other hand, arises when the increased evaporation that

China experienced a record heat wave in 2010. Thousands tried to cool off along the shore in Liaoning Province.

results from warming causes an increase in cloud cover, which tends to cool the climate by reflecting sunlight away from the earth. The overall effect of climate feedback mechanisms is almost certainly positive—that is, toward increased warming—but the magnitude of the warming is difficult to predict.

## Rising Sea Levels

Rising ocean waters are affecting every continent on the earth and pushing expanding coastal populations into ever-shrinking land areas. The rise is due to two major factors: the thermal expansion of ocean water as increasing air temperatures transfer heat from the atmosphere to the ocean (warm water occupies more space than cold water) and the melting of glaciers and polar **ice sheets** (which cover about 10 percent of the earth's land area).

Sea level rise is not a new phenomenon. Oceans have been rising since the last ice age ended, but they stabilized two to three thousand years ago. Records indicate that sea levels did not change again until the late nineteenth century, but the rate of increase since then has scientists concerned. Current measurements show a rise of about 0.12 inches (3 millimeters) per year. This century the expected rise, based on temperature predictions and projected ice sheet melt, is 8 to 20 inches (21–50 centimeters).

The glaciers that have adorned the mountaintops of the world for millenia are melting. Their disappearance threatens the supply of freshwater for the burgeoning human population. At the same time, the ice sheets in Antarctica and Greenland are demonstrating a net loss of ice (as more ice melts in the summer than accumulates in the winter). The speed of movement of some of the ice streams that are draining the Greenland ice sheet

# CASE STUDY

# THE HUMAN PRICE OF RISING SEA LEVELS

Two out of three people in the world live within fifty miles of a coastline. Rising seas will result in the loss of waterfront property and damage to low-lying towns and cities. Thermal expansion is expected to contribute about half of the sea level rise this century, with melting land ice adding the other half. In Bangladesh, more than 15 million people would be affected by a 3-foot (1 m) rise in sea level. Many of the world's major cities, including New York, London, and Mumbai (Bombay), are barely above sea level. Property damage claims and relocation costs associated with rising sea levels in these cities could be horrendous.

Low-lying islands and atolls are in grave danger of disappearing beneath the ocean waves.

Some island nations have already initiated evacuation plans. The government of the Carteret Islands of Papua New Guinea has a voluntary evacuation plan in place, as some scientists predict these islands will be uninhabitable by 2015. The social and financial consequences for families having to abandon their homes and properties could be extensive. The Carteret Islanders may go down in history as the first climate change refugees, but they could soon be followed by others. The island nation of Kiribati, for example, is considering long-range plans to relocate the entire country. What is happening to these islands may be a preview of what is to come on a larger scale as the impact of swelling oceans spreads around the world.

This photo, taken in July 2011, shows pools of melted ice atop Jakobshavn Glacier in Greenland.

has doubled in only a few years. Similar losses are occurring in the West Antarctic Ice Sheet. The East Antarctic Ice Sheet is growing in size because of increased precipitation, but not at a rate that balances the loss in the west. Antarctica as a whole is still registering a net loss of ice.

## Coral Bleaching and Poverty

The bleaching of coral reefs around the world is a consequence of warming ocean waters. Coral reefs are affected by higher ocean temperatures and higher acidity than they have encountered at any other time in the last 400,000 years. If current conditions persist, by mid-century all corals will be threatened, and three-quarters of the world's corals will face high to critical threat levels. Many of the colorful algae species that live in the outer casing of coral polyps cannot survive the high temperatures of warm ocean waters, and when they are gone, the colorless coral casing is left in a bleached condition. Without the nutrition provided by the algae, the coral polyps soon die off.

Coral reefs are rich in marine **biodiversity**, but once bleaching takes place, the diversity of these specialized marine ecosystems drops dramatically. The loss of the corals can be devastating to the income of many island communities that rely on fishing for food and trade and often have active tourist industries that are based on the reef ecosystems.

In the United States, elkhorn and staghorn coral have been classified as threatened species since 2006. In 2013 the NOAA will consider a reclassification of the corals from threatened to endangered.

## Ocean Acidification and the Shellfish Industry

The oceans not only absorb heat from rising global temperatures, they also absorb close to half of the atmospheric $CO_2$ generated by human activities. Studies now show that ocean water is changing in chemistry. The $CO_2$ is mixing with other seawater components and forming carbonic acid, the result being acidification of the ocean water. This acidity is causing thinner

Staghorn coral begins to bleach off the shores of Papua New Guinea.

shells in sea animals such as oysters, lobsters, and crabs. The acidification of seawater also affects struggling coral reef ecosystems, resulting in decomposition of the calcium-based coral casings. Many coastal communities rely on shellfish both as a food source and for their livelihoods. Climate change is adding more pressure onto the world's fishers who are already struggling due to mismanagement of their rapidly depleting fisheries.

## Desertification, Land Degradation, and Poverty

As global temperatures rise, precipitation patterns change, and many areas become drier. A combination of the lack of moisture, overgrazing, and nutrient depletion from agriculture can cause land to lose fertility and productivity. Ultimately, land affected in this way will revert to a desert ecosystem—a process known as desertification. Many of the world's deserts and dry lands are spreading. The local people in these areas, particularly in Africa and China, live in conditions of poverty. The loss of land to desertification is a further threat to their survival.

South of the African Sahara desert is a region known as the Sahel, which stretches from the Atlantic Ocean in the west to the Red Sea in the east. Covering a total area of over a million square miles, the Sahel has suffered a number of large-scale famines over the past fifty years. Desertification driven by climate change could be one of the greatest environmental challenges of this century.

## Global Food Shortages

Loss of agricultural production and basic access to food may be one of the major human costs of the climate crisis. Rising sea levels, droughts,

The seeds from these canola plants will be pressed for their oil, which will be used for diesel fuel and industrial oil.

desertification, and land degradation, all of which lead to lower productivity and higher food prices, could put 120 million people at risk of hunger, 70 to 80 percent of them in Africa, a continent that produces only 2 percent of global emissions.

An additional threat to global food supplies is the cultivation of biofuel crops. Corn and other food staples are now being used to produce ethanol and similar fuels. The amount of grain needed to make enough ethanol to fill the gas tank of a sport-utility vehicle could feed a person for one year. In the United States nearly one-third of the nation's corn crop is going into gas tanks. In addition, it takes energy from fossil fuels (largely oil or coal) to process the ethanol in the first place. Cellulosic biofuels (fuels made from cellulose, the woody structural material in plants) are now under development to avoid upward pressure on food prices.

## Species Extinctions and Human Poverty

Species that are unable to adapt quickly enough to climate change will be lost. Loss of species weakens ecosystems and leads to lower biodiversity. Weaker ecosystems have fewer options available for adapting to change. **Indigenous people** who rely on the biological resources within healthy ecosystems to subsidize their incomes or provide them with livelihoods may also find it difficult to survive. The management of protected areas and conservation programs in these areas needs to include the local people in the decision-making process to increase their chances of success. Climate change is making this process much more difficult, as managers are faced with uncertainties such as drought, fire, and invasive species.

## Infectious Diseases and Human Health

Climate change is widely expected to increase the occurrence of insect-spread diseases such as malaria, dengue fever, viral encephalitis, and West Nile virus. Rising temperatures may allow mosquitoes and other insects to increase their geographical ranges as well as their reproduction rates. The incubation period, the time needed for symptoms to develop in the victim following infection, may also become shorter. Food shortages could lead to malnutrition and weaker immune systems, which in turn would render humans more at risk for insect-borne diseases. All of these factors taken together do not bode well for human health in a warming climate, particularly in the tropics, where populations are already vulnerable to disease and where the bulk of population growth is expected to occur in the future.

## The Cost of Invasive Species

As ecosystems are impacted by climate change, they become weaker and more at risk to invasion from species that are able to survive in habitats with a wide variety of conditions. When invasive plants and animals crowd out native species, there is a change in the ecosystem balance, with a reduction in biodiversity. In addition, the local people and their livelihoods are often impacted. Hundreds of billions of dollars are lost globally from the damage caused by invasive species and the costs of controlling them. The expense is expected to rise as more opportunities for invasive species are created as a result of climate change.

## Population Growth

The climate crisis is basically a human-made imbalance in nature. The imbalance, which has been getting progressively worse for the past two centuries, is due to both the technological developments that enabled greater and faster consumption of fossil fuels and a seven-fold increase in population. It took all of human history to reach 1.6 billion people at the start of the twentieth century; in the next one hundred years the world population leaped to over 6 billion. The global human population exceeded 7 billion in March 2012 and it is expected to increase to somewhere between 7.5 and 10.5 billion by the year 2050. Having more people on

**TIME TO ACT fact!**

In the United States alone, the damage caused by invasive species and the cost of controlling them is estimated at $138 billion annually.

the planet will mean more energy consumption through the burning of fossil fuels and an increase in heat-trapping $CO_2$. What hope can there be for reducing greenhouse gas emissions while there is rapid growth in the world population? With both the human population and carbon emissions out of control, the twenty-first century will soon see temperature increases and associated impacts that could make human life impossible to sustain on the planet. Population numbers are rarely discussed in the debate on climate change, despite the fact that they are such a key component.

# Global Warming and the World Water Shortage

*Water, water, everywhere,*
*And all the boards did shrink;*
*Water, water, everywhere,*
*Nor any drop to drink.*

This stanza from *The Rime of the Ancient Mariner,* published in 1798 by the English poet Samuel Taylor Coleridge, is relevant today. A shortage of freshwater is expected in many regions as a result of rising surface temperatures. Most of the earth's water supply is oceanic saltwater—only 2.5 percent is freshwater. Seventy percent of that freshwater is tied up in the ice sheets of Greenland and Antarctica. Only 0.7 percent of the world's total freshwater is available for use, and close to 90 percent of that is being used for agriculture. Many water systems are already in trouble thanks to pollution and habitat degradation. Climate change adds yet another threat.

Higher global temperatures are causing glaciers to melt on mountaintops from South America to Africa. As a result, many rivers are expected to run dry when they are most needed—in the middle of the summer months. Populations downstream may face severe water shortages. Early springs are bringing most of the water downstream early in the season, before vegetation has fully developed. Water management, crop selection, and population control will become increasingly important in this century.

Water usage has been growing twice as fast as the population has increased over the last century, and a number of regions are constantly short of water. As the world becomes more developed, the consumption of water per person is expected to increase. Experts predict an upcoming worldwide water shortage.

The effects of climate change, such as severe drought, are being felt in many regions of the world.

## Chapter Three

# Living in the Greenhouse

**The climate in the global greenhouse**
today is the result of a number of factors: the $CO_2$ already
released, the various positive feedback loops that influence climate (such as melting arctic sea ice, which
results in more absorption of solar radiation),
**global dimming**, and the ability
of humans

to reduce $CO_2$ emissions. Humans have control over the last factor; the others are already in play. There are, however, a number of courses of action people can take to prepare for the inevitable changes to come.

## The Coast Should Be Anything but Clear

It seems inevitable that sea levels will continue to rise. Mangrove forests are important natural buffers against flooding, tsunamis, and hurricanes. They thrive in the intertidal zones of tropical and subtropical coastlines, where they also absorb $CO_2$ and store carbon. The salt-filtering roots and salt-excreting leaves of mangroves enable them to survive in the salty

Roots from mangrove trees create a sediment filter, improving water quality for the ecosystem.

# A Safe Upper Limit for CO$_2$

Many climatologists and other scientists are convinced that 350 parts per million (i.e., 350 molecules of CO$_2$ for every million molecules of atmospheric gas) is the safe upper limit for CO$_2$ in the earth's atmosphere. Observations to date indicate that at over 395 ppm, CO$_2$ emissions are well beyond the safe limit. Until the Industrial Revolution, 275 ppm of atmospheric CO$_2$ was the standard level throughout most of human history; the emissions trapped enough heat to allow humans to live comfortably. In 2012, the 2.67 ppm increase in CO$_2$ was the second highest rise on record. Methane levels in the atmosphere reached 1,803 parts per billion, up 158 percent from pre-industrial times.

According to climate scientists, CO$_2$ levels must return to the sustainable level of 350 ppm in order to avoid the melting of the Greenland ice sheet or the release of enormous amounts of methane from permafrost melting in the Arctic. Recent studies show that, even if the composition of today's atmosphere could be maintained (with no additional greenhouse gases), the earth's surface air temperature would continue to rise because of the warming commitment—that is, the warming from past human activities that has not yet had an effect. Also, many of the greenhouse gases that have already been emitted remain in the atmosphere for long periods of time and therefore will continue to contribute to warming for the duration of their atmospheric presence.

environment, where they stabilize the shoreline, prevent erosion, and provide nurseries, shelter, and food for fish. Traditional uses of the mangrove forests by local people range from firewood, medicines, food, charcoal, and construction material. Indigenous coastal peoples, including fishers and farmers, need to be included in decisions to ensure the sustainable management of coastal regions.

Coral reefs also need to be maintained in a healthy condition, since they serve as a refuge for a rich biodiversity and also because they act as a form of protection for coastlines and islands. The Indian Ocean tsunami of December 26, 2004, demonstrated the value of these natural ecosystems and the dangers of removing them for coastal resort construction, aquaculture, and beachfront tourist attractions. The tsunami killed 283,000 people in total, and 1.7 million were left homeless and displaced.

## Between Nations

The Intergovernmental Panel on Climate Change (IPCC) was created in 1988 by the United Nations Environment Programme (UNEP) and the World Meteorological Organization (WMO). This panel of scientists from all over the world provides nations with scientific information on the condition of the world's climate. International cooperation is essential since weather, climate, and the water cycle do not stop at national boundaries.

The IPCC publishes assessment reports (ARs) on a regular basis; the last was AR4, released in 2007, with AR5 expected to be completed in 2014, including the latest research and predictions for future climatic conditions. The first AR, released in 1990, established the importance of climate change as a topic and led to the UN Framework Convention on Climate Change

(UNFCC), an international treaty aimed at reducing global warming and responding to the effects of climate change. AR4 confirmed that eleven of the previous twelve years had been the warmest on record since 1850. The odds of that happening purely by chance are statistically very small. Although the previous report, released in 2001, attributed the changes in climate to human causes with 66 percent probability, the 2007 report stated that the likelihood that humans were responsible for climate change was 90 percent.

## $CO_2$ Emission Limits

The top-ten $CO_2$-emitting countries in the world in terms of total volume of emissions are China, the United States, Russia, India, Japan, Germany, Canada, the United Kingdom, Iran, and South Korea. Despite all the talk of capping $CO_2$ emissions, atmospheric $CO_2$ has been accelerating. From 2001 to 2010, the average annual rate of increase, 2.04 ppm, pushed civilization's carbon output to record levels.

One need not look any farther than the variation in emissions per capita (per person) of nations around the world to understand that lifestyle has a huge impact on emissions. Though China has surpassed all other nations in terms of total $CO_2$ output, when divided by the population of 1.3 billion people, it ranks lower than thirtieth on an emissions per capita basis. Some of the world's islands and smallest countries have the biggest per capita emissions. Gibraltar has the highest, at 152 tonnes per person. The United States is still number one in terms of per capita emissions among the big economies—with 18 tonnes emitted per person. China, by contrast, emits under 6 tonnes per person and India only 1.38 tonnes per person. By comparison, the world, on average, emits 4.49 tonnes per person.

Land-use changes, such as deforestation, have had a negative impact on the atmosphere.

# Land-Use Change

The loss of forests to deforestation, the spread of cities, expansion of agricultural and grazing land, and other human influences have altered the natural landscape. These changes have increased the level of $CO_2$ in the atmosphere, reduced carbon stocks, and affected the local and global climate. Even small changes in land use can change local patterns of rainfall and cause other changes in climate. Over 13 million acres of forest are lost each year. The ability to reduce deforestation by protecting forested areas, as well as to conserve other ecosystems that store carbon, such as wetlands and peat bogs, will determine future emissions of $CO_2$ and ultimately global surface temperatures.

# How Much Is Nature Worth?

Economics is entering into the conservation of the natural world in many ways. The Economics of Ecosystems and Biodiversity (TEEB) study is a global initiative to highlight the actual costs of biodiversity loss and ecosystem degradation in response to the fact that consumption and depletion of natural resources are taking place at an extremely fast rate. The TEEB is using experts from around the world to evaluate the economic contributions of biodiversity and ecosystems and at the same time compare them with the costs of conservation and sustainable use.

Putting a monetary value on nature and ecosystem services can be useful in the battle against climate change. If the costs of adapting to higher temperatures and all of the ensuing effects of climate change can be evaluated, it may be possible to justify the economic costs of reducing $CO_2$ emissions right now in an attempt to roll atmospheric $CO_2$ levels back to a sustainable 350 ppm.

Wind turbines provide a
sustainable, clean energy
alternative.

## Chapter Four

# Playing It Cool

Civilization has consumed an enormous amount of energy since the start of the Industrial Revolution. More than half that total energy has been used in the last two decades. Despite the fact that less than 5 percent of the world's population lives in the United States, 25 percent of the world's energy is consumed there, at a hefty usage level of 11.4 kilowatts per person. Almost half of that energy comes from burning coal, the worst carbon polluter of all the fossil fuels.

It is estimated that the proven reserves of coal are around 934 million tons (847 billion tonnes), capable of supplying the world's energy needs at the current rates of production for the next 120 years. Oil and natural gas reserves, on the other hand, could supply humanity's needs at current production levels for forty-six and sixty-three years, respectively. The question is, would humans still be able to live on a planet where all of the coal, gas, and oil has been burned and its carbon emitted back into the atmosphere?

Humans need clean energy sources that do not emit greenhouse gases. Such energy sources do exist—they just need further development and support. A sustainable civilization will need to rely on a mix of renewable energy sources. The following are some of the options available.

## Solar Power

With all of the sunlight falling on the earth's surface, capturing less than 0.02 percent would be enough to meet the world's energy needs. Solar power is the fastest-growing source of energy usage, with new solar panel installations more than doubling in 2012. One of the limiting factors for growth in this industry is the high price of making solar cells, but engineers are slowly chipping away at the cost. The second limitation is the influence of weather patterns, particularly cloud cover, and the third is the fact that solar installations do not produce electricity at night. The last is a major limitation in high-northern- and high-southern-latitude countries, where there is little daylight during the coldest months, when energy demand is highest. However, there is a possibility of solving this problem through international networking, whereby northern countries buy power from countries closer to the equator during the winter months. The most

These solar panels in Spain use sunlight to produce electricity.

successful of solar technologies is solar thermal heating, which uses the sun's energy to heat homes, and drive industrial processes. The International Energy Agency believes that solar power can contribute a quarter of the world's electrical power needs by the middle of this century.

## Wind Power

Estimating the available wind on the earth is not an easy job, but if roughly 5 percent of the wind could be captured, it would supply the entire world's current energy needs. Much of the available wind blows over the open ocean, so more and more wind turbines are being constructed offshore. Wind power produces no carbon emissions. More studies are needed to determine the effects of wind farms (groupings of wind turbines) on local climates.

Initial studies indicate that they are nowhere near the effects of greenhouse gas-emitting fossil fuels. The problem of birds being killed by striking turbine blades has been considerably reduced with the recent introduction of large turbines with slow-moving blades.

## Biopower

Biopower is produced through the burning of biomass (plant material and animal waste). It is one of the oldest forms of renewable energy and has been in use since humans learned how to harness fire. Sustainably grown low-carbon biomass has the potential to produce enough biopower to provide a significant fraction of the renewable energy needed to reduce $CO_2$ emissions. Also appealing is the fact that existing coal and natural gas power plants can be converted to run entirely on biomass. However, in addition to beneficial biomass resources, there are those that are harmful to ecosystems, atmospheric quality, and water levels. The beneficial sources include plants that do not compete for land with food crops; crop residues not valuable for nutrition, such as wheat straw; forest residues and sustainably harvested wood; and nontoxic municipal and industrial wastes. The proper development of biopower should result in lowering net carbon emissions.

In Europe and the United Kingdom, biogas is becoming increasingly popular as an alternative to fossil fuels. Produced from rotting or gasified waste, biogas can produce heat or power without venting methane, a powerful greenhouse gas, into the atmosphere. It also makes a better long-term option to the import of natural gas. The end product after the gasification is a nitrogen-rich compound that can be used as a fertilizer.

# Nuclear Power

Currently, nuclear power generates about 13.5 percent of the world's electricity. The main challenge for nuclear power in its bid for power supply supremacy is cost; nuclear power is very expensive to generate. The fact that there is also a vulnerability to radiation leaks, accidents, and terrorist attacks has led to the unpopularity of this energy source, particularly following the nuclear accident at the Fukushima power plant in Japan after the 2011 tsunami. Long-term storage of nuclear waste is also a problem, as is the fact that an enormous amount of water is required as a coolant for the nuclear reactors. Water shortages could become a limiting factor in the

Nuclear power plants generate relatively clean energy but the risk of leakage and the disposal of nuclear waste pose a threat to people and the environment.

expansion of the nuclear power industry, as future climates are predicted to be both hot and dry. On the plus side, nuclear power plants produce relatively low carbon emissions.

## Hydroelectric Power

Hydropower is as clean as solar and wind in terms of carbon emissions, but large-scale hydro projects have been known to disrupt ecosystems. As a result, hydroelectric power has fallen out of favor for a sustainable energy future. However, there may be a place for hydropower on a smaller scale, serving local community needs.

## Tidal Power

In the eighth century, the first tide mills used incoming tides to turn water-wheels to mill grain. Tidal power is a reliable nonpolluting source of energy. Building semipermeable barrages on coastlines in inlets that have a high tidal range is one way to harness tidal energy; another is by tapping offshore tidal streams. Most modern tidal operations use a dam coupled with hydraulic turbines. One of this method's weaknesses is its low capacity; another is that it is on the 12.5-hour cycle of the tides and is thus not necessarily producing to capacity at times of peak demand.

There is also wave power, the enormous energy that it takes to move ocean water up and down. The World Energy Council estimates that from 140 to 750 terawatts per hour of energy (a terawatt is a trillion watts) could be produced from the oceans via wave power from existing devices. Research is currently in progress to efficiently harness some of this vast renewable energy.

# Geothermal Power

Besides emitting fewer greenhouse gases than fossil fuels, geothermal power has an advantage over solar power because it provides twenty-four-hour output. Wells are drilled into hot rock, sometimes a mile or more deep, to access the thermal energy stored in the earth. Water is pumped into the wells, and when it comes into contact with the hot rock, it creates steam that can be used to power turbines and electrical generators at the surface. The United States is currently the biggest geothermal energy producer in the world. Theoretically, there is enough geothermal power in the earth to supply all of humanity's energy needs, but the costs of extraction prohibit accessing most of it. More studies are needed to assess the risks of drilling deeply into the earth's crust. There is some concern that the drilling and injection of water may trigger seismic activity (earthquakes).

# Algae Power

Oil exists today because 300 million years ago, algae and other plants filled the seas and swamps. Now scientists are hoping that the slimy green slick can do it again, this time in large ponds created on infertile land. The beauty of the process is that algae absorbs $CO_2$ and is powered by the sun through photosynthesis. Algae power produces five to ten times more energy molecules than crop biofuels. The biggest hurdle is the cost of production.

# Clean Coal Technology

Coal, a combustible black sedimentary rock, took millions of years for nature to create from plants and algae trapped at the bottom of swamps, and covered by layers of water and dirt. Heat and constant pressure eventually

# Dung Power

What do you get when you have elephants, rhinos, and wild boars all in one place? You get a lot of animal dung. The Toronto Zoo knows only too well. The zoo animals produce about 1,000 tons (907 tonnes) of dung and other organic waste every year.

The Toronto Zoo management has plans to build a biogas plant nearby that can turn all that animal manure into clean electricity and heat. Bacteria in an oxygen-free environment consume the dung and excrete methane. Burning the methane gas powers turbines that produce electricity, or alternatively, the gas can be cleaned and sent directly into natural gas pipelines. The zoo power plant will also be able to burn through the waste from local restaurants, grocery stores, and other nearby industrial facilities to generate heat and electricity for five thousand homes in the surrounding community.

created what is now called coal. When burned, coal emits sulfur dioxide ($SO_2$), mercury, nitrogen oxide, particulates (particles that float in the air), and carbon dioxide. Ecosystem and environmental damage, particularly to nearby ground and surface waters, is common in the process of coal mining. Traditional coal mining and traditional power generation through the burning of coal are dirty processes from start to finish.

**TIME TO ACT fact!**

Coal-fired power plants are the cause of 25 percent of the world's carbon dioxide emissions.

Almost 50 percent of the coal burned in the United States is used to generate electricity. Power plants have ways to reduce $SO_2$ emissions using equipment known as scrubbers. Clean coal is a term that refers to methods used to reduce the $CO_2$ emissions (and other greenhouse gases) from the burning of coal for electrical power. This technology is still under development. Carbon storage involves the capturing of $CO_2$ from the emission sources and somehow storing it permanently, possibly underground.

The Sossusvlei is a salt pan found in Namibia in Africa. A lake forms at its center during years of bountiful rain.

## Chapter Five

# Should We Engineer the Climate?

Geoengineering is the large-scale manipulation of the planet to counteract the effects of climate change. Despite its liabilities, some think that geoengineering has the potential to stave off some of the impacts of climate change. There are a number of scientific schemes, some more feasible than others, for bringing the earth's climate back into check.

# Iron Fertilization in the Ocean

Iron is used by all plants in photosynthesis. When iron is in short supply, cellular growth in phytoplankton is limited. Iron fertilization is the intentional addition of iron to upper ocean waters to stimulate phytoplankton growth. Some scientists suggest this technique as a means to gather and store atmospheric $CO_2$ in the deep ocean, as phytoplankton take in carbon in life but then sink with it after they die. There is no consensus on the effectiveness of the technique, however, and much debate rages over its possible negative ecological effects. For instance, a recent study showed that the iron can stimulate the production of toxin-producing algae, which can poison some marine species. The scale of an iron fertilization experiment required to create a significant uptake of atmospheric $CO_2$ would have to be enormous, and therefore, any negative impacts would also be significant.

# Solar Radiation Management (SRM)

This geoengineering theory suggests that by spraying aerosols into the upper atmosphere, the reflectivity of the clouds below will be increased and sunlight will be scattered, the result being that the amount of solar radiation reaching the earth will be reduced. There are natural historical events that support this theory. Mount Pinatubo, when it erupted in the Philippines in 1991, sent enough particles of sulfur dioxide into the stratosphere to cool the earth for a period of time. Other consequences are as yet unknown, other than less precipitation and less evaporation. Some claim that, at a cost of $5 billion to $10 billion a year for a short-term program, SRM could be a fast and cheap solution—cheap by geoengineering standards, at least.

Steam and ash explode from Mount Pinatubo in 1991. Particles thrown into the stratosphere from this eruption briefly cooled the earth.

## Carbon Sequestration

Many developed countries are pinning their hopes on storing excess $CO_2$ either in the ground or in the ocean. On the plus side, removing $CO_2$ from the atmosphere by "scrubbing" it out has the advantage that the results would be observed immediately. The problem is that the removal would have to continue for decades, even an entire century, to be effective, and there is always the danger of leakage. Another consideration is the source of the energy to scrub the $CO_2$. Would it be another carbon-spewing power source?

> **TIME TO ACT fact!**

After a period of severe drought starting in 2004, Australia's five largest cities are now spending $13.2 billion on desalination plants to ensure that they have water in a warming world.

# Bioengineering

Some proposed solutions to climate change advocate the manipulation of living organisms. The Great Green Wall (GGW) of Africa received approval in early 2011, with pledges of up to $3 billion by international development agencies. Conceived of by eleven countries located on the southern border of the Sahara and their international partners, the GGW is a planting project intended to limit the spread of the Sahara desert into the Sahel zone, the transition between the Sahara in the north and the African savannas in the south. The GGW initiative intends to plant a belt 9.3 miles (15 km) wide of drought-tolerant trees and plants across the entire African continent in the Sahel zone. As well as preventing desertification and slowing climate change by lowering temperatures and absorbing $CO_2$, the wall of trees and vegetation is expected to provide food and nontimber resources to the local people and thereby help to alleviate poverty and promote political stability in the region.

# Concerns and Geoengineering

Most geoengineering solutions suffer from three common concerns. The first is the unpredictable side effects of implementing some of these plans. As weather and climate are variables, to truly observe the effects, a large, long-term experiment needs to be implemented. If the side effects are worse than the cure, a full-scale experiment could create a global food shortage or other major problems. The second concern is the astronomical cost of undertaking engineering solutions on a planetary scale. These installations would have to be maintained long term; if the engineering were to be removed, the underlying problem of greenhouses gases in the atmosphere would be worse than ever. The third concern, and probably the most important of all, is that these designs may delay action toward the reduction of carbon emissions and lull the world into a false sense of security. As more and more $CO_2$ is pumped into the atmosphere, the impact of climate change worsens, and the scale of the recovery required grows larger.

Scientists and researchers are striving to develop practical and affordable clear energy solutions. The solar panels shown below are a good start.

## Chapter Six

# The Future Is Now

*You must become the change you wish to see in the world.*
—MAHATMA GANDHI

**Climate change is a sensitive topic,** one that arouses passionate arguments about our relationship with the natural world. Discussions are taking place in almost every nation as scientists, governments, and individuals come to grips with the magnitude of the climate crisis.

Despite the diversity of nations and cultures on the earth, everyone shares the same atmosphere. It is important that nations come to realize that, as is often the case in a crisis, there is opportunity for great growth and positive change. The climate crisis could provide the momentum for a radical shift in how we relate to the natural world. Our role could change from that of consumers of natural resources to one of stewardship, a role that assumes the responsibility of steering civilization toward a future of clean energy and living in harmony with the natural world on a healthy planet.

The changes required to reduce our collective carbon footprint provide many opportunities for new inventions, new technologies, and new careers. A Japanese inventor named Akinori Ito, concerned about the accumulation of plastic waste, created a machine that reduces plastic back to oil without emitting any $CO_2$ and at an electrical cost of less than 20 cents. This product clearly demonstrates that an empty bottle, a discarded lunch box, or a rain hat is not really plastic—it's oil! This brilliant invention also shows us that there *are* solutions to the environmental and climate change–related "problems" that we find ourselves in. It just takes a little innovative thinking.

## What You Can Do

One of the ways that individuals and families can make a real difference is in their choice of automobiles. Electric cars top the list of low-carbon footprint vehicles. They produce zero emissions from their tailpipes. The total reduction in $CO_2$ emissions for electric cars of course depends on how the electricity used to recharge them is generated. Some industry experts predict that by 2020, a full third of global car sales will be "green" vehicles.

Electric cars getting their batteries recharged on a street in London, England.

Hybrid vehicles (also called hybrid electric vehicles) reduce emissions but maintain flexibility by combining an electric motor with an internal combustion engine. Their carbon footprint is higher than that of strictly electric vehicles, owing to the burning of fossil fuels. Vehicles that run on ethanol or natural gas are lower in $CO_2$ emissions than petroleum-only vehicles.

There are vehicles in development that are powered by another promising technology—fuel cells. Fuel cells generate electrical power without any pollution or greenhouse gas emissions. They run on hydrogen gas, and the only by-product is water. The main drawback right now is the cost of making the fuel cells and the hydrogen fuel, and the size of the unit required to run an automobile.

In February 2011, two "eco-sportsmen" drove 3,000 miles (4,828 km) across Australia in a car powered largely by the wind. The 440-pound (200 kg) vehicle is a kite surfer—a wind turbine and an electric car rolled into one. Batteries charged by the wind turbine power the electric engine, which can also be simply plugged into an electrical outlet. The total cost of the journey was about $16.

Of course, one of the best ways to reduce vehicle emissions is to walk, ride a bike, use public transportation, or share vehicles through carpooling. Fewer vehicles on the road mean less $CO_2$ in the atmosphere.

If you choose to stay at home and telecommute to work or just want to make your home more energy efficient, there are a number of things you can do. Check with your electric utility company about a "green" energy option. Installing a programmable thermostat will ensure that heat and air conditioning are not wasted when they are not required. Also, dress warmly at home so that the thermostat can be reduced a few degrees. Turning off lights when they are not being used and replacing bulbs and showerheads with energy-efficient ones can also save energy.

Replace petroleum-containing products in your home with sustainable alternatives. Consider how efficient your appliances are and whether replacing them with more energy-efficient models may save money and carbon emissions at the same time. Your family might want to investigate switching to a solar water heater or a photovoltaic system. Adding insulation and airtight doors and windows can reduce energy needs year round.

The food you eat can have a big impact on your carbon footprint. Buying locally from farmers' markets can save trucking, packaging, and refrigeration energy. Growing your own home garden can save even more.

Once you start to think about living sustainably, you will meet many people of like mind. Consider joining a local environmental group and helping your community make good energy-saving choices. Support and elect politicians who understand the science of climate change and the need to reduce $CO_2$ emissions.

# Glossary

**biodiversity**  The variety and number of plant and animal species in the world or in a given habitat.

**biosphere**  The world viewed as the sum total of all living organisms and their ecosystems.

**carbon footprint**  The amount of carbon dioxide emitted by an individual or by a transportation or production process over a given period of time.

**carbon sink**  Anything that absorbs more carbon that it releases, such as forests, oceans, and soil.

**CFC (chlorofluorocarbon)**  One of a family of gaseous compounds used as refrigerants, cleaning solvents, and aerosol propellants. CFCs have been linked with the destruction of stratospheric ozone and therefore with an increase in solar radiation reaching the earth.

**climate feedback**  The response of the climate system to direct effects imposed on it by natural or human influences, either in the form of positive feedback, which increases the effect, or negative feedback, which decreases the effect.

**global dimming**  The reduction in sunlight reaching the earth because of particulate matter in the air produced by automobiles, coal-fired power plants, and other industrial activities.

**greenhouse gas**  An atmospheric gas such as carbon dioxide, water vapor, methane, nitrous oxide, or ozone whose absorption of solar radiation has been linked to climate warming (greenhouse effect).

**ice core**  A tube of ice extracted from a polar ice sheet or mountain glacier.

**ice sheet**  An ice layer covering a land area larger than 20,000 square miles (50,000 km$^2$).

**indigenous people**   A people regarded as original to a particular geographic area.

**infrared heat**   Heat produced by sunlight that radiates away from the surface of the earth and into the atmosphere. Because greenhouse gases can trap infrared heat, they interfere with this radiation.

**invasive species**   A nonnative species introduced, sometimes deliberately, into an ecosystem; it can harm native plants, animals, and microbes and cause economic disruption.

**troposphere**   The atmosphere's lowest portion, where most of the earth's day-to-day weather occurs.

# Notes

## CHAPTER TWO

p. 16, "The number of . . . almost eighteen a year.": R. A. Kerr, "Is Katrina a Harbinger of Still More Powerful Hurricanes?" *Science* 309 (2005): 1807.

p. 17, "It became the . . . $81 billion.": Richard D. Knabb, Jamie R. Rhome, and Daniel P. Brown, "Hurricane Katrina," Tropical Cyclone Report, August 23–30, 2005.

p. 17, "In Europe in 2003 . . . 35,000 deaths.": Shaoni Bhattacharya, *New Scientist*, October 10, 2003, www.newscientist.com/article/dn4259-europeanheatwave-caused-35000-deaths.html.

p. 17, "Meteorological data shows . . . temperature is accelerating.": J. Hansen, R. Ruedy, M. Sato, and K. Lo, "Global surface temperature change," *Reviews of Geophysics* 48, (2010) RG4004 29 PP.

p. 19, "This century the expected . . . 8 to 20 inches (21–50 cm).": IPCC AR4 (2007), www.ipcc.ch/publications_and_data/ar4/wg1/en/ch10s10-es-8-sea-level.html.

p. 21, "Coral reefs affected . . . threat levels.": "Reefs at Risk Revisited" (2011), World Resources Institute. Washington, DC, www.wri.org/publication/reefs-at-risk-revisited.

p. 26, "In the United States alone . . . annually.": D. Pimentel, L. Lach, R. Zuniga, D. Morrison, "Environmental and economic costs of non-indigenous species in the United States." *BioScience* 50 (2000): 53-65.

p. 26, "The population . . . by the year 2050.": International Data Base (IDB)—World Population, Census. gov. 2010-06-28, www.census.gov/ipc/www/idb/worldpopinfo.php.

p. 27, "Only 0.02 percent . . . used for agriculture.": IPCC AR4, 2007. www.ipcc.ch/publications_and_data/ar4/wg1/en/faq-5-1-figure-1.html.

## CHAPTER THREE

p. 31, "Observations to date . . . beyond the safe limit.": http://co2now.org/.

p. 31, "In 2010 . . . 800,000 years.": "Carbon Budget Highlights" (2010), www.globalcarbonproject.org/carbonbudget/10/hl-full.htm#AtmosphericEmissions.

p. 31, "The second most important . . . preindustrial times.": World Meteorological Organization Press Release No. 903 (November 24, 2010), www.wmo.int/pages/mediacentre/press_releases/pr_903_en.html.

p. 32, "Many people died . . . homeless and displaced.": "Magnitude 9.1—Off the West Coast of Northern Sumatra," U.S. Geological Survey, http://earthquake.usgs.gov/earthquakes/eqinthenews/2004/usslav/#summary/.

p. 32, "The AR4 report . . . since 1850.": IPCC Fourth Assessment Report: IPCC AR4 (2007), www.ipcc.ch/publications_and_data/ar4/syr/en/mains1.html#1-1.

p. 33, "From 2001 . . . record levels.": "Acceleration of Atmospheric $CO_2$," National Oceanic and Atmospheric Administration (NOAA), http://co2now.org/Current-CO2/CO2-Trend/acceleration-of-atmospheric-co2.html.

p. 33, "Though China . . . per capita basis.": $CO_2$ Emissions by Country. http://co2now.org/Know-GHGs/Emissions/co2-emissions-by-country.html.

p. 33, "By comparison, . . . per person.": "World carbon dioxide emissions data by country," *The Guardian* (UK), www.guardian.co.uk/news/datablog/2011/jan/31/world-carbon-dioxide-emissions-country-data-co2#data.

p. 34, "Over 13 million . . . each year.": "State of the World's Forests" (2012), Food and Agriculture Association of the United Nations, Rome, http://www.fao.org/docrep/016/i3010e/i3010e00.htm.

## CHAPTER FOUR

p. 37, "Despite the fact . . . per person.": "$CO_2$ Emissions from Fuel Combustion," (2010 Edition), International Energy Agency, Paris.

p. 38, "It is estimated . . . 120 years.": "Where is coal found?" World Coal Association, http://www.worldcoal.org/coal/where-is-coal-found/.

p. 38, "With all . . . energy needs.": International Energy Annual 2006. World Electricity Data, World Net Geothermal, Solar, Wind, and Wood and Waste Electric Power Generation (Billion Kilowatthours), 1980–2006. www.eia.doe.gov/iea/elec.html.

p. 39, "The International Energy Agency . . . this century.": "IEA sees great potential for solar, providing up to a quarter of, world electricity by 2050," International Energy Administration press release May 10, 2011.

p. 39, ". . . if roughly 5 percent of the wind . . . current energy needs.": Jefferson W. Tester et al., *Sustainable Energy: Choosing among Options* (Cambridge, MA: MIT Press, 2005).

p. 41, "Currently, nuclear power . . . of the world's electricity.": Nuclear Power in the World Today, www.world-nuclear.org/info/inf01.html.

p. 42, "The World Enegy Council . . . from existing devices.": World Energy Council. Publications, Survey of Energy Resources (2009), Tidal—the Resource, www.worldenergy.org/publications/survey_of_energy_resources_interim_update_2009/tidal_energy/default.asp.

p. 45, "Almost 50 percent . . . generate electricity.": *Innovations for Existing Power Plants*, www.fossil.energy.gov/programs/powersystems/pollutioncontrols/.

p. 45, "Coal-fired . . . carbon dioxide emissions.": Coal and Electricity, http://www.worldcoal.org/coal-the-environment/climate-change/.

## CHAPTER SIX

p. 54, "A Japanese inventor . . . 20 cents.": United Nations University: Plastic to oil fantastic, http://ourworld.unu.edu/en/plastic-to-oil-fantastic.

p. 55, "In February 2011 . . . about $16.": Martin Love, "Eco-car drives like the wind across Australia," *The Guardian* (UK), February 27, 2011. www.guardian.co.uk/environment/2011/feb/27/wind-powered-car-crosses-australia.

# Find Out More

## Books

Anderson, Dale. *Al Gore: A Wake-Up Call to Global Warming.* New York: Crabtree, 2009.

Challen, Paul. *Migration in the 21st Century: How Will Globalization and Climate Change Affect Migration and Settlement?* New York: Crabtree, 2010.

Hanel, Rachel. *Climate Fever: Stopping Global Warming.* Mankato, MN: Compass Point Books, 2010.

Nardo, Don. *Climate Crisis: The Science of Global Warming.* Mankato, MN: Compass Point Books, 2009.

Nardo, Don. *Climate Change.* Greensboro, NC: Morgan Reyolds, 2010.

Spalding, Frank. *Catastrophic Climate Change and Global Warming.* New York, NY: Rosen, 2010.

## Websites

### Action for Nature (AFN)
This group emphasizes action that benefits the natural world. Every year AFN hosts the Eco-Hero Awards, which recognize the achievements of young people in environmental initiatives. There are two age categories: eight through thirteen and fourteen through sixteen. www.actionfornature.org/

### Energy Action Coalition
This site is a hub, for more than fifty youth-led environmental and social justice groups. Working together since 2005, the Energy Action Coalition supports a clean energy future and environmental sustainability. http://energyactioncoalition.org/

### Kids Ecology Corps
This site encourages hands-on presentations and eco-action programs for students from prekindergarten to grade twelve. Subjects include water conservation, tree planting, energy conservation, and climate change. You can volunteer to help out with some of their activities, get involved in beach clean-up, or join a public reach campaign. www.kidsecologycorps/

### Kids vs. Global Warming
Started by a fifteen-year-old named Alec Loorz, this site provides guidance to help young people become involved in the climate change crisis. Visitors can learn how to do school presentations, get active in their community, or take a leadership training course. Communication is one of the keys to being effective in the battle against climate change. www.kids-vs-global-warming.com/Home.html

# Index

Page numbers in **bold** are photographs, illustrations, and maps.

# About the Author

**Stephen Aitken** is fascinated by the natural world and its remarkable diversity. He is the author of many books for young people from third grade to high school, written for publishers all over the world. Aitken is a biologist and senior editor of *Biodiversity,* a peer-reviewed science journal, and executive secretary of Biodiversity Conservancy International. He is a vegetarian, does not own a car, and tries to keep his carbon footprint as close to his shoe size as possible. The author's studio in the beautiful Himalayas of India provides shelter for ants and spiders, baby geckos, and an odd orange-eared mouse.

For a complete list of books that Aitken has written and illustrated, please visit www.stephenaitken.com.